Poems from Oby

By the same author

The Broken Places
A Doomsday Book
The Colour of Blood
The Night of Stones
A War Quartet
The Burning Cone
Collected Poems, 1958-1970
The Orlando Poems
Shrapnel
A Poet's Year
In the Hours Waiting for the Blood to Come
Buying a Heart
Poems of Love and Death

My Scotland

Noah's Journey
Jonah and the Lord

The Transformation
The Samurai
The Survivor
The Seven Witches
The Born Losers

The Penguin Book of Sick Verse
The Penguin Book of Animal Verse
Poetry 1900-1975
The Penguin Book of Victorian Verse
The Falling Splendour
The Book of Cats

Poems from Oby

George MacBeth

Secker & Warburg
London

First published in England 1982 by
Martin Secker & Warburg Limited
54 Poland Street, London W1V 3DF

Copyright © George MacBeth 1982

British Library Cataloguing in Publication Data

MacBeth, George
  Poems from Oby.
  I. Title
  821'.914   PR6063.A13

  ISBN 0-436-27017-X

Printed in Great Britain by
Redwood Burn Limited
Trowbridge

Contents

Acknowledgements

Some of these poems have appeared in: *Ambit, The Countryman, Encounter, A Garland of Poems for Leonard Clark, The Listener, The London Magazine, New Poetry 7, The New Statesman, Pacific Quarterly, The PBS Christmas Supplements 1980* and *1981, Places, Quarto, Stand,* and *The Times Literary Supplement.* One was broadcast in *Poetry Now* (Radio 3), and one was a Sceptre Press pamphlet. To the editors of these magazines and anthologies, and to the Sceptre Press, my acknowledgements are due.

Foreword

The parish of Oby, pronounced Ōby, lies about nine miles
from the sea, in a part of Norfolk so nearly encircled by
water as to be called the Isle of Flegg. The manor of Oby
was mentioned in The Domesday Book, but now the manor-
house and the church have gone. Only a few scattered farms
and cottages, and the former rectory, remain. I bought this
rectory, together with two and a half acres of weed and
woodland, in November 1979. These *Poems From Oby,*
written largely since moving, are the fruit of a new
involvement with the countryside. There are themes
handled before, in *Poems of Love and Death,* as well as in
earlier volumes. But the treatment is now, I hope, more
consistent, and less diversified by comic and performance
and experimental elements. There is also, I think, more
optimism than usual, surprising perhaps in a poet approaching
fifty. The reason may only be — but what is the word "only"
in this context to mean? — the luck of settlement, finding a
piece of land to feel secure on, and someone to live there
with. I am grateful for this good fortune, and offer
Poems From Oby as a down payment on what is owed.

This Evening, Lisa

Since I am come, in my mid time, to where
The nettle glories, and the common weed;
And I must find some borrowed scythe to bare,
And rake the leavings of my former need,

Which was a wife, and home; and, since I tire
Of walking aimless, and I crave some place
To part the embers of a homely fire,
Such as is yours now, my committed space,

I walk tonight through silence, and watch smoke
Circle above the chimneys of your aims
In quiet air; and, hearing the far stroke
Of human axes, I renounce cold games

As my intent; and, by the sound of blades
Through fallen wood, at distance, I defer
To country ease. The gathered ranks of spades,
And forks, under our awning, and the stir

Of supper from the kitchen, teasing sounds,
And smells, to urge the palate, these all blend
And mount a fresh insistence, and with grounds,
Frail grounds, but good, to make my lone life end.

I choose for sharing, and I share with joy
This twilight, as I hear your sleepy child
Whinge from the other room. What would annoy,
Before our match, is taken now, and filed,

As what may need adjustment, but is mine
To hold and pay for, and is life's, and true.
And I look out, drawing my ancient line
Behind our cobwebbed glass, grateful for you.

Somewhere

In all those rooms, no light
Unfiltered by the trees.
Only the broken spears
Of sunlight through smudged glass:
And windows dimmed with webs.

Across the road, thin sheep
And a church behind its yews.
Weeds to a crumbled wall
And an undergrowth of grass
Great roots of beech lay bare.

Indoors, the musty smell
Of old wood drying through
And forgotten food left out.
Sour milk in open cups.
Dead bread along a board.

There are many beds unmade
In that exotic house.
The remains of passengers
Whose lives have fallen in
And thrown them out to the sky.

In the attics, time has knelt
And driven holes through jars.
The scum of paint in tins
Tells of a former care
That blistered in the halls.

A foot of green slime swills
In the cellar by the stairs.
Brick arches built for wine
Are in water to their knees
And toads now croak for port.

Here, on the barren floors,
The vapid slap of soles
Remainders gaiety
To the drone of testy flies.
Even the cat's foot slurs

In unfurnished corridors
And the hinges of the doors
Creak with a hidden weight.
There is black, unmanaged soot
On the ostrich of each grate.

Whoever used these rooms
Has abandoned them to the air.
Air, and the stink of rats.
But outside, the long gallery
Of chestnuts rustles leaves

And the garden gives away
What the mansion chose to lose,
A sense of grand repose.
The stately lines of pride
From a rectitude of prayer

Are simplified to the shape
Of a summer's afternoon
Where growth is an elegance
And people come to read
In the shadow of old trees.

Walking, and loving these,
In the gentle wind and the heat,
May be all that remains to aid
Or obliterate the decay.
It seems so, this summer's day.

Lament for a Fledgling

Down on one knee
I dug your grave in earth
Under an apple-tree.

And, by the root,
I threw away your nest
To lie with shells and fruit.

Now, in light rain,
I stoop beside your corpse
And lift it out again

Limply, from where
You stretched, and died. Sleep sound,
Pheasant, near all this air

You were born to own
And shadow with your wings.
You need no funeral stone.

Only the croak
Of a few crows from the wood.
And a far-off axe's stroke.

Only the bark
Of our spaniel from the house.
And the quiet breeze of dark.

One day, some gun
Would have shot you from the sky
In the glare of the autumn sun.

You died too soon
To know the force of lead.
Accept the gentler moon

On your closed eyes
And dream of brakes instead
From which your mother flies.

Free of her fate
You rest in fertile soil,
Marked by a scrap of slate.

Let no rough hound
Ever shake it with his foot
Or mar your burial-ground.

And let my spade
Scatter your grave with soil.
And some recompense be made.

My Parents' Things, the Yielding

Taken from where they live,
And carried through the day a hundred miles,
Or more: and eased from their old folds,
Or crisp elastic bands;
Buff telegrams, white wedding-cards, a will;
Patents for pit-props, and a pulley-block;

These lingered in their hands,
And were touched often: each brought grief, or smiles;
And what it gathered, and now holds —
This blurring negative,
That roll of school reports, this lawyer's bill —
Far from the moment it was keyed to lock,

Remains in light; in golds
From corn and evening splattered on my hill;
In time, as in this fluttering clock;
And on my neighbour's lands,
White harvest; so what these prepared, and give,
Grows peaceful, changing, under Norfolk tiles.

I feel pain, where they spill,
And lay them flat, with reverence, in files,
In leaves: but with no twinge of shock.
My time to move, and sieve,
Has come. To settle feeling where it stands.
To garner all my scars, like fruitful moulds.

Ripping Up Lino

Ripping up lino from a rotten floor,
I let the boards breathe. Here dry rot runs rife,
And must be stopped. When I drove through my knife,
The timbers crumbled, and the skirting tore.

Now I look down on dulled flat zones of oak,
Wondering whether damp still strives to rise
From its buried well. Our house is of some size,
And bounded by a ditch, and this might soak

Through soil and brick in summer to each joist,
And bring more rot in. So I worry here,
In pleasant autumn, while the ditch is clear,
About what signs to look for, from things moist,

Or gathering puddles. When the ditch is full,
And floods to five feet in its winter yield
Below the beeches, and beside the field,
Shall I be able to withstand their pull,

Those tides, those winter tides, that seek to break?
The deep, hard surge of anguish as it's thrown
Along the wormed earth, that was overgrown,
And now stands barren, and is bare to ache

In the cold wind? I wonder, and I pause,
Sheathing my penknife, with my fate in hand.
I have to take a step, and make a stand.
I need the pressure of a proper cause,

A home. The needs of family and place.
A thing to tackle with a risk, and hope,
Quite gradual, but uphill, like a slope
That leans towards a level, for a base.

There I could set a small lake, with an urn
And finial, to top this life of care
And standing idle, with a thing to stare
And wonder at. And go from, and return.

That would be plenty, in my country grounds,
And worth the hindrance of this hidden mould
Under the house, from nature, and her hold.
Something like profit, from my water bounds.

Five Horse Chestnuts

    I saw them shine. They were the first,
      This cooling year, thrown hard and bland
Along the littered road in Pembridge Square,
      Amidst the pointed leaves. And there,
Caught by the sunlight, on my open hand,
I felt their power, with a kind of thirst.

    It comes in colour. Then in sheen
      And polish, to impair, and move,
Part plausible as elegance, or age,
      A kind of rich, hand-crafted rage
For keeping living to some furnished groove,
And, more, for being ripe now. Now I lean

    Their five shaped honest backs to rest
      Along your rosewood writing-desk
We bought in Hampstead. And its brass knobs, bright
      Although near winter, take the light
Out of the foolish West. And, Hardyesque
In gloomy sun, like nipples on a chest,

    They throw the gleams back. I salute
      Such loyal redness, glowing down.
Times changed for us, and nights grew darker. Yes,
      When I screwed tight my trouser-press,
One night, beside you, in your dressing-gown,
Our ailments verged on autumn, and bore fruit.

    You filed your suit. And I drew back,
      And, in that drawing, found relief
From what was mine. My illness, or my guilt,
      Never expired on what we built,
Nor even from the fungus of your grief
That ate through reason. Like a kind of lack,

It fed on dying, and prepared its price,
    In sores that festered later. Well,
It had its parallel, for me, with what
    I knew before, my war-bred knot
Untieable by trying. Truth to tell,
I think all loved ones die, but mine die twice,

    And stain my mind. Things grow too plain.
    I leave my shelled nuts for you, sure
Of your approval of their glowing needs,
    Their polished rounds, their glittering seeds,
Their purpose to create, and to endure.
Through dying leaves, and shells, to bloom again.

    It would be so for me. The power
    That, rising, settles from the tree
And scatters uncupped energies. That, white
    Through thawing soil, emerges light
And flexible, as branches. This, for me,
Is what I wait for, through each wasted hour,

    In hope. The power still to smile
    Through days of dimming to the dark
Where dreams and absence violate the brain,
    And vex its cadence. To retain,
From all those flowering chestnuts in the park,
One branch of sticky buds, transformed by style.

A Poem In Doubt

I have a dream this year,
Which is a rectory sold
To friends: but when the auctioneer
Has finished, what they own and hold

Has passed to me. I mean
The large rooms high and clean,
And gardens blossoming with flowers,
And beds of fruit-trees. There the powers

Of darkness and the night
Sweep down through owls in flight
And fill the barns. The common blades
Of axes are as blunt as spades

And do no work. The hand
Of someone unseen moves
His trowel through, and, lightly panned,
Scatters the seedlings into grooves.

This was a dream, I hear
A voice beside my ear
Report. That house you dream of dies.
Look for a place of proper size

For your small needs. Neat walls
Down which no fungus crawls
And eats: low ceilings, whence no heat
Leaks out, and leaves you frozen feet,

And workless hours. I see
Close to the kitchen door
One shed for tools: and one dwarfed tree
Beside the gate. You dreamed before

Too often of that grange
Where you could so arrange
All things to meet the needs of grace
Appropriate to a country place.

Draw in your horns, I say,
And turn that house away
Where all your energy would fail.
Find something more on your own scale.

That was a dream, too. Guilt
In common clothes of brown
Came through the double doors I built,
And sneered, and pulled my great house down.

Katrine's Kittens

Behind the fire-guard, against a spade,
Near to a green tray, in the inglenook,
By a bellows, and an iron, they were laid.
I heard their tiny mewling. And I took
A pair of cushions to make bricks more kind,
And propped her back. But she was of no mind

For luxury, or sloth. She licked the head
Of one just born, and purred. Thus reassured
By that huge rumbling, he looked much less dead,
And raised his blind eyes, and was black, and cured.
They were five now. Like mice against her side,
Mouths to her nipples. And not one had died.

I turned, and smiled at you. Life had begun
For another handful, on a day of blue
And cloud-flecked sky, in the September sun,
And these were Librans, mutable like you.
The mother moved round, and I watched her rest,
Five small heads heaving on her tired breast.

You turned away to type, and I to write,
And the morning darkened. By the ancient bricks,
Turning to check, I saw another sight,
A mass of jelly. And I counted six.
The sixth small kitten came too late, and cold,
And needed help. When he was one hour old,

You warmed him in a duster. By the sink,
Along the Aga, cleaned his mucused nose,
And felt him stir. A sudden mouth, round, pink
And raw, opened, and then his high voice rose,
And yelled for help. Hours later, now, I say,
Six kittens are alive still, born today.

Their Flying Dreams

Today you piled a barrow high with bricks,
And cleared the grate, and lit a blazing fire.
Beside your flames, we stretched our cracking hands,
And hunched in sheepskin. And I felt at home.

Outside, our gutters may have harboured leaves,
And muddy rain replaced the promised snow.
But here, beneath each stone Victorian rose,
I spread my booted legs, and felt a lord.

In the empty library, I saw my books
Rise in their rosewood case, and stoop from shelves.
Urns over walnut watched the distant yews
And shutters marked the floorward swoop of glass.

Time would remove this dusty patina
From boards no longer young, but still laid true.
And space would shrink the measured stretch of pine
To something darker, to a table's glare.

I warmed, and rose, and walked towards the wall.
Shaking the curtain loose from its brass rings,
I took the thinning cloth. And then a moth,
A huge one, with four hawk's heads, rose and flew.

It hit the window like a wetted sheet,
It seemed, until I loosened the glass catch,
And let it through. It flew towards the South,
Into what sun was left, and left me safe.

It seemed an omen. I could live and work
In these firm rooms, and shake them loose of life
Into the burst world, if I wanted, free
To shatter daylight, and leave me my dues.

Air to the winged things, and to me my house.
A proper bargain. And the slackening rain
Seemed for a moment to admit more light
Out of your fire, to confirm this bond.

I saw the future, and our children stand
Mirrored against those blackened, further trees
In the cold December night: and, hand in hand,
At ease with us, gather their flying dreams.

One Gone, Eight to Go

On a night of savage frost,
This year, my smallest cat,
The fluffy one, got lost.
And I thought that that was that.

Until, late home, I heard,
As I fumbled for my key,
The weak sound of some bird.
He was there, mewing to me.

There, on the icy sill,
Lifting his crusted head,
He looked far worse than ill.
He looked, I'd say, quite dead.

Indoors, though, he could eat,
As he showed, and fluffed his tail.
So much for a plate of meat.
So much for a storm of hail.

Now, by the burning grate,
I stroke his fragile spine,
Thinking of time, and fate.
Lives go. Men don't have nine,

As kittens do, to waste.
This lucky one survives,
And purrs, affronted-faced.
But even he, who thrives

Tonight, in my cupped hands,
And will grow big and grey,
Will sense, in time, the sands,
And fail, and shrink away.

Typing a Novel about the War

I pause in the sun.
I level my L.C. Smith against the entrenched line of
    trees at the end of the field.
The angle of light changes three degrees on the page.

I try again.
Surge of the patterned iron, the brass shift-lever, the
    yellows of the letters' eyes.
Dust and oil.
The frictive smoothness.

I try again.
Smell of gas from the blue cylinder invading
    my nostrils.
I breathe.
Warmed for a moment by sun filtered through the
    Maltese cross of my house.

I die forwards.
Reflected back.
The sun moving west to my right.

I watch the double ribbon advancing through the gates, fed
    by the rusting drums onto the page.
I hear the ratchet of the roller bar, locked into place
    with its flattened screws.

Trees into words, it seems to say. Words
    into trees.
And the grinding lubricity that macerates as it cures
    shatters and eats at the paper it tells how it was.

I pause.
The sun moves, and I feel the glorious warmth
    on my face.

Snowdrops

The first day of this month I saw
Their active spearheads. Dry and raw

They rose from grass, beside my pond,
In a white stockade. And now, beyond

Far evergreens, more gather, and
Advance on dead ground. Dour they stand,

As if numb earth depended on
Their stolid hold. And what has gone,

Or will go, when they give, means time.
Time to be emptying ponds of slime,

Time to be slow, time to work hard.
I see them thicken, yard by yard.

These are the first of our strong flowers.
Before the spring, or April showers,

They teem with loyalty, and fight
For a place in the sun. Static in flight

Their icy lances pierce with green
Last year's downed leaves. I touch one. Clean

And moist upon my reaching palm,
I feel its energy, its calm.

Thoughts on a Box of Razors

bought at a Stalham sale

I
For two pounds, they were mine. The price seemed right.
I thought of Housman's shiver, as he shaved,
And open sorrows that might cut the skin.

One razor curves beside me, black and clean.
It seems to swoop, when closed, as though in flight.
The hollow, bird's-beak-sectioned blade's engraved.
I touch its coldness, anxious to begin,

Watching the thirteen others as they grin.
Men's tender bodies are what razors craved.
I sense their famished hunger, their sweet bite,
Their glitter in ebony, obsessed, obscene.

And yet this glitter, with its power to stun
That seems so Japanese in these, looks trite.
It takes me back to Sheffield, and what's done.

II
Suppose I try to focus on just one.
This German GBNG, flecked with rust
And dated 1918, 's caught the sun.
Spread out across my page, its vague V-thrust

And hooking nose bring Dorniers to mind.
My war, that was. I hear old engines drone,
And civilians dying, with no testament signed.
That blitz was mine, I feel it as my own.

Others have carried razors, cold like this,
And stropped them sharper on strong leather thongs.
I touch my German friend. Its rustling kiss
Across my finger thrills like Chinese gongs.

I see the owner was E. Mann, my name.
My mother had one like this, much the same.

III

I go too far. I've jammed one in a churn,
A butler's cleaner for a carving-knife.
You shove a handle, and twinned rollers turn
And clear the blades of grease. In all my life

I never saw one till eight months ago
At an Aylsham sale. I bought the next I saw,
And cleaned it up. I use it now with dust
Of emery powder that's already in.

It's weak, but it works, with knives. A kind of crust
Will come off surfaces, and make things show.
I thought I'd clear the razor of some flaw,
But it caught inside. The blades of knives are thin,

A razor's upper section's far too thick.
This made the movement of that whole drum stick.

IV

Now I lay ten in a circle. Each has teeth,
Like cogs in an alarm-clock, and a groove.
As if relaxing, edges are in sheath,
And out of sight. They make a ring of steel,

Whose rim is ivory, whose hub is bills,
Or beaks. I mean the hooks you shift them by,
And make their sharkness arch with. As it moves,
You feel the irony. It eats and chills.

The irony that glisters in each eye,
Brassy and raised, is part of why they wheel
Into such penguin swimming forms. They fly
Only when open, vicious by the keel

That clears by inches the sea floor of time,
And leaves for grief deposits, bloody slime.

V

"Napoleon" seems much skinnier than the rest.
A trifle stiff-backed, and a smidgeon marred.
In the middle of his blade, he has a nick.
Old Nick. They might have called him that, for fun,
In Sheffield, England, where they carved his kind,
Those cutler brothers, John and William Ragg.

I see them in their sweat-shop, bony crags
Like stalwart men, with Elbas on their mind.
They slaved, like Mr Stokes, like everyone
Who listened for the cold alarm-bell's click,
And took home hands grown calloused, and bone-hard.

These built Napoleon, by their chimney-breast,
And sent him far from Sheffield, to shave chins.
I tap their dread invention on my shins.

VI

Razors need razor-like precision. These
Don't quite have that. This boxful leans on rhyme.
I see the brook of recollection freeze,
And feel the cross of parting, like a crime.

I could abandon rhyme, though. Force a sly
Sixth-line decision to be less exact.
A sort of gear-change, as it were, in fact.
That would be fluid, like a flow of thigh.

I don't suppose I'll do it, though, nor try.
Good rhymes can cut you. They can make you cry.

Remembering does that, too. So when I
Remember blue Gillette, and rusting blades,
A kind of guilty subjugation shades.
I see my father's car, and cases packed.

VII

Wearing these memories, in their common flight,
I take up three fresh razors, heavy ones,
All black. I need the heft of weight tonight,
The drag of solid iron, like a plough's,

To upheave my brain. Ideas hinge and flee
At the solstice of a poem. They earn space
By how they touch me. Seconds out, I see
The reaching hands of grief, and her blank face.

The razors wait like rifles, nose to tail.
Like strips of hardened sword-blade, in a pail.
Like knights in armour, for their holy grail
Going to war, in coats of khaki mail.

Turning, I hear the sound of English guns.
I see my mother's tears. I touch her blouse.

VIII

I touched her blouse again when she was ill,
Feeling the curve. Razors have that, well-wound
As if around some foreign hill. Great scythes
Don't hold the same allure. Scythes rake the ground

While razors float. They take our skin for tithes,
Winged surgeons. At our faces, with their fists,
They scrape and till, until the tissue breaks,
And leaves wide acres open to bare cysts.

The mother's curve, though. Is it this that makes
The elegance of swords from old Japan?
The simple shape of Time, drawn as a man?

I don't know. There's a straightness in their rule,
Razors. When I was nearly twelve, at school,
I used to want a razor that would kill.

IX

I never got one, though. I bought my first
At a garage sale in Saratoga Springs.
It's lying stiff, bone-yellow, much the worst
For wear, while all my rest make rings

Around it, on that empty cabinet
Whose lacquer top I'm using for their ground.
It's ominous, a tale of warring kings,
A nightmare game. How ten bright shiners rose

And trapped a colleague on their killing-mound.
Somehow I don't suppose the rest would set
Into a pattern slighter than I chose
If any sliced his neighbour into bits

And screeched away. I wonder, though, if it's
More razor-like to savage with no sound?

X

Once you get fantasy, what's left to say?
You get sheer viciousness, a misty sheen.
Imagine some girl murderously neat,
Stiff as a fish-bone sticking in your throat.

She takes a sharpened razor. To make sure,
She sharpens pencils. To make doubly sure,
Until those hexagons shed flakes of cones
She sharpens. Those are fir-tree's, these are hers.

She sees her man walk home from Stalham, gay
In his gaiety, and randy as a stoat.
It isn't easy to be quite so mean,
Even as she is, like a bitch on heat.

She does it, though. Cover the man with stones.
Bury this John Clarke's razor, with his bones.

XI

No true disciple of the modern world
Would aim to buy a cut-throat still to use.
Even a safety razor might seem odd.
Those brushes in the window, that arcade

Off Piccadilly, seem to stand for show.
Collectors might accept one, nicely curled
Into a smooth maroon case. Years ago
When all men lathered, in some louche decade,

It might have frightened you to read the news
Of a Sweeney Todd, a-swivel in your chair.
It wouldn't quite have marked one as a clod
Not to be shaved well, but, in good repair,

A gentleman kept razors. That was life.
As necessary as a decent wife.

XII

My father lost his, in a time of strife,
Long after he had gone. In middle age
My mother knew the worst, and what she said
Stays with me now. The Royal Hospital

Had instruments laid out on moving trays,
Like razors. Did they shave the nightly dead,
And lay them empty in each well-made bed?
This is the memory that slowly slays,

The sight of screens. What happens with the knife
Behind those frills must happen to us all
In years to come. And it's good cause for rage,
That frictive rage against the dying light

I feel seep through these handled, broken forms,
And rake in agony, like icy storms.

XIII

Downstairs I hear the heater moving. Tired,
I know it's after eight, and time to eat.

You will be cooking, standing by the stove,
Slicing potatoes, carrots, from your crate.
The table may be laid. And silvered blades,
Planted for eating, ordered by each plate.

They'll take my mind away from these retired
And scandalous old razors. Quite as neat
As razors, in much straighter lines, knives store
Bold energies of peace, of summoned awe

Our quiet house provides. By natural law
I ought to honour this deliberate grove
Of stainless trees. But, no. Knives have it made.
I prefer razors, they do rougher trade.

XIV

In sadness, I feel inspiration fail.
I bought these cut-throat razors in a box
With a wireless, and a metal case for coins.

I didn't need them, I just like old blades,
And things to keep things in, symbols of loins
Psychiatrists would say, the spike and hole.

But it's really more than that. I like these locks
Along the money-case, and on my chests,
Even if they don't close. I like the shocks,
The tingling brinks, of razors. In this house,
I falter sometimes when I touch your breasts.

I have to try again. To keep things whole,
In all we do, it helps to think of raids,
And live with a Sheffield edge. Wholeness is frail.

The Little Ghosts

I wake, early.
Shallow dreams wash at the curtains of my mind.
Something disturbed the plush tenor, the Norse barque,
        of sleep.

What was it?

Buried iron, they say, makes ghosts restless.
Somewhere a spine or a pot forgotten under earth has turned
        its lock of tears, and the great yacht of memory and desire
        floats up, freighted with Viking bones and Victorian blood.

Then, at near to five, the dawn chorus begins, an external
        prickle, an itch of light, from the garden.
My calf, besieged to a throbbing mound by a dispossessed flea,
        afflicts me again.

That's it.

I watch the grey blur of my squared pane, haunted by the
        X-ray of a tree.
To the right, at the far edge of my land, the high ground
        conceals gold rings and perambulators, or only, perhaps,
        the rotten, dismembered segments of day.

I think of the two dead hedgehogs, whose energy I buried at
        the delta of the wood.
These charismatic irritations in my skin, perhaps, are the
        little ghosts of their urge to live.

They haunt me still.

The Renewal

The need to find a place always returns.
In Richmond, where my eighteenth century bricks
Fashioned an avenue to stable skin,

I built a proper house. At Holland Park,
That fleece and leather took their comfort from,
I tried another, in another way.

Both worked. And what the simple martyrdom
Of wanting some position broke for sticks,
And set in place, held back the creeping dark.

I turned there, in my darkness, on my beds,
In tiny rooms, alone, and with my wives,
Or girls who passed for wives. And all my burns

From being lonely, and unsatisfied,
Flared in the silence, like a sheen from tin.
I waited, and, while waiting, something died.

Then, in the heat of Norfolk, I found you.
You brought the sun, through darkness, to my hives,
The bolted iron to my crumbling sheds,

You changed the whole world's shape. Your power grew,
And I, in feeling that, wanted some place
More generous for it than those gentle homes.

I needed somewhere with a flirt of grace
To match your fervour for long acreage.
I found it, here at Oby. Naked space

Over the cornfields, and the next-door farm,
Contracts to an oasis with great trees
That north-east winds can ravage in their rage

And leave still rooted and serene. In these
I feel the sweep of beech-wood, like an arm,
And something deeper, in our copper beech.

That brings a birthright in its massive reach,
A sense of giant time. Seeing it blaze
In widespread feathering, I feel the past,

The creak of longships on the Caister shore,
The swing of mills beside the easy broads,
And something closer, groping slow, at last,

The pleasant rectors, knocking croquet balls.
I take their heritage, and what it pays,
And vow today to make its profits pour

Through founded channels, in my well-kept grounds,
As growth, and preservation. Nothing falls
Or sings, in this wide garden, but its sounds

Calm me, and make our full liaison rich.
So my dream-Scotland grief was noble in
Will drag its graves beneath these grounded urns,

And stake its base in watered Norfolk clay,
And Kinburn be reborn, as what it was,
And my grandfather, and our Springer bitch,

Both live, in their own way, and like it here,
And feel the rain and sunlight on their skin,
And no one tell apart, which one is which,

The dream of former grandeur, and the firm
Everyday presence of our daily lives.
This is my hope, and what these lines affirm.

Passing Water

Standing above the bowl
Of elegant porcelain
And waiting to pull the chain
I feel the memory tug
And the tears come back again.

When I was four months old
The evening ritual
As with many a mother's child
Was washing me in the sink
And then towelling me dry.

One night, a young visitor
Who was humoured to hear me cry,
And wanted to understand,
Asked if she might be allowed
To hold the boy on her knee.

You tell the story well
In your scribbled letter here
I can hold and touch in my hand.
I read it through when it came,
And I cried, and then I smiled.

Naked below the towel,
Rinsed, and a little pink,
The immaculate child lay safe
In the surrogate mother's arms.
I feel your particular joy,

Being six years old, and proud,
And I know your shame, when I peed
All over your beautiful dress.
I can see the disbelief stir
Into a mire of need

When your curiosity drained
To a gentle bitterness.
You were too young to believe
In a boy so insensitive
He could void his feelings in mess

And consign your frock to the soap.
My mother, you say, knew better
Than to let you go without hope.
She said what she said, and her words
Were comforting, passionate.

Never you bother, dear.
If he's a remarkable man
You can write and tell him how
He passed water on your dress
When he was one year old.

You said you would. And now,
Fifty years afterwards,
You have honoured what you said.
Honoured the living dead,
And given one precious thing

To their representative,
Their ageing, surviving son
Who treasures what he knows
And remembers what he can,
And will take your story to heart.

It is holy water that flows
Out of the body's ends,
And a little was given from mine.
It touched you, and made us close,
Baptised by a kind of soiling

Into a hope that will last
For years. Though we scarcely met
At an age that could learn to refine
Each other's lives, and their cast,
By this water's touch, we are friends.

A Letter to Lisa

It might have been a pack of cigarettes,
A matchbox, or a flattened envelope.
It isn't what it was, that gently sets
And focuses. It isn't that, I hope.

Others have written words on wrinkled tin,
On prison walls, on lavatory tiles.
A few have scattered fragments in a bin,
Or paged their anguish into gathered files.

I know one girl who burned her grief on skin,
And laid her agony in patterned smiles.
It isn't what it was, or what it's in,
Or where it goes, that shadows, and beguiles

In broken words, in cries for cancelled debts,
In open wounds where tempered feelings grope.
It isn't those. Not always. Not the pets
Of pampered vehicles that cringe to cope.

Others have chosen those. You took some card,
Just any card your tear-flushed eyeball scanned,
And bent your crayon to what seemed most marred
And least available to understand,

Your need. And yet your hint of suicide,
I wish that I can kill myself, seems less
Than what you pencilled on the other side:
The underbelly of your bitterness.

O, I can write these lines in decent pride,
And not feel too much sense of pain, and mess.
After all, children have been known to hide,
Even to denigrate, their happiness.

I wonder, though. It takes a heart too hard
For any praise of mine to find quite bland
I want to go back to my Daddy, starred
And blotted by a seven-year-old hand.

Women Who Visit

I own the whole house. Nude on boarded floors,
Or clothed in cane chairs, I admire their busts.
Gliding with honeyed ease through scented doors,
I turn their lurid sleeps to dreamy lusts.

This is my fantasy. In shoes and gown,
I mount one visitor across the stairs,
Another in her room with blinds still down,
The first one as she combs her moist crutch hairs

With sickly fingers on a cork commode.
This is the life. I love it. In her skirt
Of turquoise Thai silk, where her boy-friend strode,
I whip the first until she screams she's hurt,

And squirms away, and comes, on icy tiles.
I rise and wash. Watching your flushed face now,
As you sleep exhausted, belly down, with smiles
Of a relished pleasure lighting up your brow,

I tune my fantasy to bitter fact.
These are the landscapes that ignite desire,
The Turners of the mind that still attract
Even at sunset, with declining fire.

Others may need them. And I may, one day,
In ancient relish for some burning crone,
Wither in spending, as I strive to pay,
And thank my thinking, I can die alone.

Spirits

Watching the window into the future
Which is Television,
In a cooled Edwardian room,

I heard one cry, in the distance,
Like a thin blade sticking in wood
Or a rusty hinge.

For a long time
I listened, wondering if I dared
Go out into the darkness

And look for it. At twilight,
I had seen several swoop
Like anchors, out of the eaves.

And once
I had halted, faced by an Austrian eagle
Hovering black on grey a foot or two from my eyes.

I went into the dairy
And out with a blue torch
Towards the beech-wood, in the East,

Where the sound came from.
It was louder there
In the night. A kind of frenzied sawing.

A few feet down
In the ha-ha
I flashed the beam into the branches.

But nothing moved.
Nothing except the grey kitten
Who had followed me out.

I went in, disappointed
And still afraid. I could have gone further
Into the blackness,

Called their name.
Instead, I came indoors
And sat down at the kitchen table,

Beating, you said,
The devil's tattoo, unconsciously,
On the scrubbed pine.

Against Melancholy

The blend of ecstasy and filth
In smell of drains, in robin-song,
Offers the kind of fruitful tilth
In which a poem might grow strong.

I lie here on the Arvon mains,
In evening sun, and think of this:
Enjoying fruit of redbreast brains
And odours of uncycled piss.

And watching two cats hunting mice,
One on a post, one on the grass,
And finding all this rather nice
Though very sore upon the arse.

At home in Norfolk I report
On life and luck with weary grace
Reading my Cowper with a sort
Of glumly eighteenth century face.

Down here in Devon Betjeman
From glossy covers gives me hope
That I might scan like a witty man
And quite forget the way to mope.

It happens. And I rise, renewed
From smells and sounds of mingled spoil,
Going in to eat my pie, imbued
With a sense of well-rewarded toil.

Thanks to the robin, thanks to drains,
And thanks to T.S. Eliot, who
Gave good advice on crossing strains.
Yes, thanks to T.S. Eliot, too.

To Preserve Figs

for Iseult

Go up the whitewashed ladder, by the wall,
        And you'll find seven pounds
    Of them, half-ripened, on the tree.
        The rest were low
    I picked before. They wallowed free
        Near to the ground's
Welter of nettles, apples, weeds. I know,
    You'll have to take care. You might fall.

But there are plenty, seven pounds I'd say,
        Still floundering heavy, green
    And solid in the August air,
        And you can reach
    Them if you climb. So go up there
        And get them, keen
As fig-juice in your envy. Gather each
    Into your fingers, let none stay,

On the branch. It makes a metaphor for lust,
        This grasping for the rounds
    Of unripe figs that ooze their juice,
        Their sperm. It burns,
    That juice, and has no helpful use.
        You'll live with mounds
Of severed energy, with jaded urns
    Whose milked white necks you'll have to trust

Through all your life. It's best you learn that soon.
           The acid in the fruit
      Prickles the world with its pain
           And nothing breaks
      The dour addiction of the brain
           To what may suit,
Or spoil. So watch your mother while she makes
      These tractable. Take up a spoon

And help. Three times they boil, and have to steep,
           Then boil again. Three times
      It always has to be. So let
           Them dry in trays
      In your burning oven. Go and get
           A sugary slime's
Blandishing oil. In winter, black to your gaze,
      Like whales from arctic ice, they'll leap.

The Field, Tomorrow

I wanted the bare field out there to be mine.
Each day, at my typing, I saw the smooth line

Of the sycamores, breaking the sweep of the grass
To the farm and the river. I saw the sails pass

Far away, white and simple, where yachts moved at Thurne.
And I looked down, in pride, at my nearest stone urn.

From that urn to the sycamores, this was my land,
With the wide breadth of Norfolk stretched gold on each
                                                    hand.

I had space, in my dream, and six acres to keep.
I had grass for my garden, and twenty new sheep.

It's all over. The field has been sold, to my friends,
And the dream of broad acres, all hope of it, ends.

At the auction I bid high, too high for my good,
And I'm glad that I missed it, at that price. I should

Have been forced into borrowing, bound to the shape
Of solicitor's ropes. But it still feels like rape

To see horses, brown horses, that other men own
(In my mind they seem galloping, sculptured like stone)

Out there in my bare field. I touch them, and weep,
And remember my dream, and the slow-moving sheep,

Their cold, lovely fleece, and their beautiful eyes,
And their mouths, low and cropping, surrounded by flies.

The Green-Eyed Monster, Jealousy

I never knew my eyes were green
    Until you told me so
This morning, and I rose and looked
In the wardrobe mirror. Well, they looked grey,
        I'd say,
Morose, perhaps, and rather cooked,
And with no phosphorescent glow

Such as the lustre, or the sheen,
    Of peacocks, or the slow
Light-slither of oil. They seemed quite booked.
They rolled, as if to mark the sway
        Of pay,
Or alcohol, or being rooked,
Or feeling borne down by some blow.

Brown-eyed for fifty years I've been,
    And I'd say, really, no
You're wrong. They're not grey-green, but crooked
In a kind of undetermined way
        The play
Of character allows to seem dull, hooked,
But with a swift kingfisher flow,

Pouncing to weed itself. I mean,
    Jealousy has to go
Like mildewed barley, badly stooked,
Or winter corn grown mouldy, hay
        That may
Only by goats, as grass, be brooked,
Or straw, grief-stricken, that won't grow.

The Hornet

October brought the last one of the year
And laid it sleeping on your window-frame.
It stood for winter, and the failing game,
The end of something, and death coming near.

Drowned in a jug, with cardboard slid across
To keep it under, it sleeps always now,
Its warrior's head bent sideways, like a bow
Made to an enemy, for the mortal loss.

I see its body, simple as a cone
Of pine or Douglas fir, cypress or spruce.
It has no meaning, scarcely any use
Except to make more precious all we own,

The last of life, and living in this place,
Year in, year out, with what we have and hold,
Great barns, and trees, and somewhere to grow cold
And die in, when the time comes, with some grace

And a kind of honour, free from bitterness
Or rancour, and not losing elegance
At the last, as this dead hornet's final chance
Left it a scoop of terror. That, O yes.

November at the Piano

for my mother

Not able to play, I touch your keys with the unskilled tips of
    my fingers, feeling a tune. The music
Echoes to the edge of the world. From the kitchen, the smell
    of a good dinner prowls, encountering my nose.

All senses coagulate. Holding the yellowed strips of ivory
    down, I squeeze out a last
Resonance from the hammered strings. It sings like a dying
    fly into corners of dust where vases

Of laurel abandon their petals. The delicate flavour of
    chord upon discord settles. The savour of hope
And melancholy in the balance of high and low that is all I
    can manage mingles. Outside the long window,

November is gathering force. In the sweat of the gale, my
    great beech-tree is sewing the grass with fire. I dwindle
Into another mould, a minute excrescence of tiny sound as I
    plunge my finger onto

A sharp note, slicing it off, like a breath of onion, or dry
    smoke. I remember your hands
As I touched them once, over sinks and baking bowls, and in
    power along such keys as these. I salute

Your competence in my ignorant feeling. I use my nose and
    my ears, under my hands, to arouse my mind.
I shall never play the piano, as you could play it, or cook,
    as you could cook. I can only

Suffer the sense of trying, hearing the sound, smelling the
    odour. This first November here
In my chosen Norfolk, what seems to matter is to ground
    your place in my echoing house, and to blaze your skills.

Mother, I need to remember, I need to feel. I have only these
    three senses to reach and hold
You with. Let me see your face in the fallen leaves. Let me
    taste your blood in the apples down from our trees.

Like Guilt

for Orlando

You were there, always.
Even when I never saw you, I thought about you.

Eleven years go into the mincer.

You were carried by Tabitha to your Eton, under the
    springing broom, in our garden.
Every day she brought you, and every night
    took you away.

Like Death.

Now you are gone yourself, before me, to that dark,
    twisting road through the shrubbery.
Whiskers quivering for something familiar to
    see and smell by.

I think of wet rabbit, sliced each morning to
    chunks for you.
I remember frozen coley, steamed warm each evening, and
    cooled for your mouth.

But for your food, what could we do for you?

I never saw you ill once, even when the vet ripped
    that fur-wrapped bone from your stomach.
And we lived again, cancer pushed for a moment
    back to the wings.

It was kidney damage that killed you.
That and pleurisy, like your forerunner, twelve
    years ago.

I heard today.
I touch my wife's letter again, here in a
    Norfolk you never saw.

My wife, once.
My cat, once.

You were the end of our marriage.
You were the son we never had.
The most beautiful, most tender thing in the world.

And the guilt never dies.

The Attack

For half an hour you never spoke
And then you screamed, *the light, the light,*
And shook, until your whole head broke,
Hot in my arms, things seemed so bright,

And you were talking like a child,
Singing in Spanish, and you said
Are you my Mummy? slurred, daft, wild,
And Lisa's face went soft and dead.

Hard to believe now, hard to bear
Driving to Yarmouth through the rain
And smiling at the doctor there
While your behaviour went insane.

It isn't now. That strange disease
Has filtered back, and left you here
At home, and human, on your knees
With toys, beyond the reach of fear.

Whatever took you, gives you back
And I am thankful, though confused.
I watch your mouth, lest it grow slack,
And all I've done seems half accused.

Yuletide in Norfolk

The long-ships drove up the Bure, and the horned men were
     there to rape and to burn,
Seeding their names, Rollesby and Billockby, Fleggburgh,
     Clippesby and Thurne,
Ashby and Oby. Our church roofs came from the rot of each
     oak-warped stern.

But the Nazarene grip was strong. The surge of energy in
     the whoring blood
Settled for the purpled moan of the organ, the heifer
     chewing her cud,
And the cart with its thwarted axle broken and stuck in
     December mud.

I drive to the service at Clippesby, a mile along
     sugar-beet-sodden road.
My lights throw up the parishioners, whipped by the
     Christian goad
And the hope of Heaven, their faces pinched by a cold,
     unearthly woad

Into shapes of bread and wine. Their archangels gloat and
     wither on spruce,
Bald winter's fuel from Norway. The tied surplice is
     shaken loose,
And the paean rises, the bitter semen of prayer squeezed
     like a juice.

Nothing can alter the sounded heritage from the
     throbbing brine,
The keels lifting above the waves. Let humility
     be divine.
All arrogance is human, the black pride of the Vikings
     is mine.

The Flyers

In the bad days I had five animals, five toys.
An owl made of red tufts, an owl with brown wings, a
    little white owl, and an owl made by The Society
      for Distressed Gentlefolk,
and a dog, a Skye terrier, whose name was Dougal.

Why these, I never knew.
But they flew.

Night after night round Richmond in the dark, for
    fun, and to take care of things.

But if I needed them, they were back.
I never knew them gone, or saw them landing, and was
    frightened by it.

They were always there, staring out it seemed into
    the lighted streets, from the window sill.

Every night I came home at two in the morning, quiet
    and guilty, I arranged those five totemic apologies
      on their sill.
Every morning they were there, to be seen.

Sometimes, even, she woke in the half-darkness, and murmured,
    happy it seemed and sleepy, *the flyers.*

And that was enough.
Just enough, in the bad days, to keep the world going.

This morning, after what she and I never had, or rarely,
    sexual intercourse, you said you could see a badger
      outside in the field, through the window.
Joking, to wake me up.

I said the little badger, the fur one who lies all
    day on our bed, went outdoors at times, but
      we never saw.

It brought them back.
The flyers, and what they meant.

I write these lines here as you take your bath, alone
    now for only a moment, sad for what never was.

Commemorating the flyers.

The Owl, in a Kind of Isolation

I write for those who need no voice,
The élite and lonely, and the proud:
Like that one hovering by the ditch
Whose world is all the field of choice
Where mice and sparrows cry aloud

In the means of his claws. I watch him, rich
And yellow in the evening sky
Quartering his manor for a kill
As medieval as a witch
And lethal as a weasel. I

Who drive in low gear, following, still
Wonder what he is seeking there
Cold in the fallen mud and leaves
With gathered blood that has to spill
And feathery tenderness laid bare.

I know the hunger that bereaves
To satisfy some ache of need
Not for food only, but for power
In insolence of rustling sleeves
Above the abandoned, where they bleed.

I turn beside the standing tower
Of what once crumbled, years ago,
And left a chancel, thatched and spare
Against the wind, sensing them cower,
His victims, nine good feet below

The inexorable wings. Down there
In the ploughland, upright now and strong,
I see his great eyes fixed on mine
Through glass that he might smash and tear
In uncivil rage. I have been too long

Away from passion, and the line
Drawn between waiting and the claws
That reach for what they want. He turns,
Knowing this too, and with no sign
That he might care, follows his cause.

Draft for an Ancestor

When I was young, and wrote about him first,
My Uncle Hugh was easier to hold.
　　　　Now, in my age, at worst
　　　I take him by some outer fold
Of what was his. His Humber, by the door.
　　　That, at the least, if nothing more

Creates an image of his prosperous time
And thumbs in waistcoats to suggest their power.
　　　　I hear tall glasses chime
　　　And clocks from walnut sound the hour
As they drive to Derby, where their horse will lose.
　　　At last, it seems, men have to choose

What traits in relatives they will to raise
To the height of models, awkward, fey, or strong,
　　　　And there arrange as praise
　　　For the unhooked soul, keen to belong
To its family, some tree of love and grace
　　　In which there blossoms no mean face.

I feel this drive. As years go by, it grows
And I want an ancestry of heroic mould
　　　　Fit for a world that knows
　　　How to accept the subtly bold
Who grasp at shields and leaves with a sprig of wit
　　　And honours their effrontery with it.

So Uncle Hugh, that self-made, stubborn man
I see in photographs, and hear in my head,
　　　　Provides a flash of *élan*
　　　To the ranks of my more sombre dead
And, startling, floods their quarters with his brash
　　　And flighty Scottish kind of dash.

The Closet

for Joanna, before the cancer operation

This little closet, where I come to pray
　　And read, is where I ought to sit
　　　　And write, not kneel.

　　I like the barrenness of it.
　　　　It makes me feel
Monk-like, and I can sometimes be that way.

　　　　It has two rooms.
　　The outer one fronts on a yard
With a fine view of grass, urns and an ash.

　　The chair I put in there, though hard,
　　　　Seems rich and brash,
The jug and bowl cold marble, like a tomb's.

　　　　But, through the door
Of simple sycamore, the rusting latch
　　Creaks onto whitewashed walls,

　　　　Odours that catch
　　The breath, and something subtler, more
Like history's own air, that roughly shawls.

　　　　The window there,
High up, looks over nothing, it's opaque.
　　The floor is common brick, but cold.

　　It might look sad and bare,
Somewhere to void the intestine's inner fold,
　　　　Or stow a rake.

Once it was potting-shed. Once where
Men eased their bowels
Under that lively, fitted bench of pine:

A place for trowels
And bulbs, things moist and quaint and spare,
And now a sort of oratory, of mine.

I have a book,
A kind of altar, panelled seat, or splat,
Raised from a bedstead, gold and high

(Oddly pre-Raphaelite, at that)
And candles. I
Suppose I liked the Oxford Movement look

Their kind of tapering purple gave
To the narrow space
At noon: and something more, their light at night.

I made my nave,
Anyway, in this icy inner place
Run west: and that seemed almost right.

A sort of decorator's game
It was, at first,
And then a portent, now a kind of need.

Each day I go, and, in the name
Of some compulsion deeper than a creed,
Think of the worst,

And even force my hands to hold
Each other in the shape for asking aid,
And, from the floor

Beneath my legs, feel earthy cold
Creep up through tweeded flesh, and elbows laid
           On elm rubbed sore.

          Tonight, not there
But in the house, alone, as it grows dark,
      I hear the Easter Sunday wind

          Howl in the bare
Thin April beeches, feeling I have sinned.
    And what seems huge, and dim, and stark,

    Is you still downstairs here, too ill
To see all this as mattering: fearful, soon
           To be in pain

    Perhaps: or rise and live again,
Grateful for these ten days, as for a boon,
         But waiting, still.

The Scapegoat, the Bat

The other closet, where we found the bat
Lies under laurustinus, to the right
Of a bewildered yew. Early at night
After you pulled loose plaster from the wall
I heard a creaking, found him lying flat
On a pile of rubble, hardly alive at all.

It seemed so, then. But later, going back
In expectation of a bat quite dead,
With canvas mussed, in our Victorian shed,
We found an absence, only brick and stone
And something sadder, like a sort of lack
Framing the wych-elm, slack there on its own.

That furry stranger, with the massive ears,
Who couldn't manage on the monstrous ground
According to the books, had made one sound
Of famished grieving, anger, or reproach,
Then clawed his route up, sloughing off his fears
Of dangling naked, like a deco brooch,

And hung in secret, once again, away
From human contact, and the touch of grief.
He must have felt a curious relief
As I did, to be high, and out of reach.
There wasn't very much that we could say
Finding him gone. Our apple, with no breach

From nipping teeth, sat rotting in the dust.
No smell, or trace of droppings, left a sign
To show our visitor had been hurt. Fine
Twilight was filtering silence, air was chill,
And the door-latch felt rough with ancient rust.
Our bat had flown. Our guilt had drunk its fill.

This Morning, Lisa

Rising to look on England through the rain,
And waiting for our guests, I feel at ease,
Knowing the best: and what seems large and plain
In this long week of worry, and will please

In other weeks, more full of weight and joy,
Is all that works to keep things here in state,
And a kind of loving. If I should employ
Less obvious words to raise and celebrate

What shouts from every beech and rafter, fine
In Georgian window-squares, and growing dense
In high Victorian mouldings, and the line
Along our outdoor dado, you could sense

My reticence, my indoor hope. And so
It is, an indoor hope, that, still, the worst
Will yield like broken nettles, and will flow
Into a lake of deep relaxing. First,

In these thrawn verses, I commemorate
All that has been a glory to our kind:
Meals in a place of honour, friends and plate,
And something left for cats, beyond mere rind.

Next, I approve of working, and our woods,
Those great trees in the distance, and the wind
Flooding new growth with rain. There, in dark hoods,
And moving slow machines, the weeds were thinned.

Last, in remembering that, I speak your name
Inside my head, the source and depth of all,
And, crossing through lost lines, I say my aim
Is to uphold my house. May it never fall.